Found

Volume 1:
Coming Back Home

Found

Volume 1:
Coming Back Home

Courtney Schlosser
The Nest Collective

FOUND
VOLUME 1: COMING BACK HOME
Copyright © 2025 by Courtney Schlosser. All rights reserved. No part of this book may be reproduced, stored in a retrieval system, or transmitted in any form or by any means — electronic, mechanical, photocopying, recording, or otherwise — without the prior written permission of the author, except for brief quotations used in reviews or scholarly works.

Published by Courtney Schlosser, The Nest Collective LLC

ISBN: 9798291445037

This is a work of poetry. Any resemblance to actual persons, living or dead, is purely coincidental.
This book is a personal interpretation of the author's evolving relationship with God. It is not intended to speak on behalf of the Catholic Church or offer theological authority.

To my husband, James

The one who, through all of our adventures, has brought me closer to God. I will love you forever.

Foreword

This book is a collection drawn from over ten journals written across more than a decade. These pages hold poems, reflections, letters, and glimpses of life as I've lived, grieved, loved, and slowly grown closer to God through it all.

The idea of this book first came to me in 2017 as a fragile thought. I didn't think it would survive. Even now, it still feels delicate. But by grace, encouragement from my now-husband, support from close friends, and a quiet whisper that never left, it finally made its way to life.

I began writing in 2014, shortly before my eighteenth birthday, after the sudden and tragic loss of someone I loved deeply. A horrific car accident left me in shambles right before I was supposed to leave for college. I spent countless days and nights in my bedroom alone, trying to wrap my head around it. Writing became a way to cope. It was a way for my heart to speak when I had nothing to say. What started as letters to him turned into letters to myself, then into poems about loss, love, friendship, family, and the quiet beauty in ordinary moments. Looking back, I see I wasn't just writing to myself or the people I lost. I was writing to *God*. And He was listening the whole time.

God was always there, but I didn't recognize Him. For most of my adult life, I was trying to follow

Him, but I lacked direction, discipline and understanding. I hadn't spent much time reading the Bible or familiarizing myself with His story. I only prayed when I needed something. I only went to church when I had to. I felt far from Him. I *was* far from Him.

Everything began to shift when my husband and I went through catholic marriage prep classes while we were engaged. It helped us tie the knot with God, literally. Before we got married, we started making space for God in our everyday lives. We began praying at dinner time. We started attending mass on a weekly basis. I sought out books and other ways to continue my education and faith independently as well. Later, after becoming a mother, I felt an even stronger pull to dig deeper into my faith. Slowly, I began to rediscover Him. My relationship with Him grew stronger and stronger. This book is part of that unfolding. My hope is that, through these pages, you might sense God's presence in your own story, even if you've missed it before.

I believe you should meet God on your own path. You should be excited to know Him, proud of the life you're building, and eager to share your journey with Him. I pray you find your way to God in a way that feels true and real. And maybe, just maybe, this book can be a small light along your path to find Him and be *Found*.

Found

Volume 1:
Coming Back Home

This is for You

Tell me all that you do have.

Tell me how the wispy vines
wrap around your house,
like a soft hug from the garden of Eden.

Tell me about your beautiful fireplace,
how it crackles and radiates warmth
throughout your living room.

Tell me how your kitchen holds
delicious basics
that long for the kneading of your hands and mind.

Tell me how your soft bed
calls you each evening for a good night's rest,
only to unfold new opportunities for you
the next morning.

Fill my ears with the beauty of your life,
the little and mighty joys,
and everything in between.
And then,
tell me how you're unsure of Him,

tell me He doesn't deserve your time.

Tell me how it's unfair,
how you are the victim in your story.

Say it,
as you taste the sweet syrup
in your daily iced coffee,
as you dress yourself for the day
in clean, warm clothes,
and step into a world
that is not yours.

Riddle me this,
what has He robbed you of
that you did not come to Him for?

This book is for you.
Because all this time,
it's not that He has taken from you,
misled you or been absent.

It's that you've walked right past Him.

The End of a New Beginning

I knew it was time to move on from this book
when I realized I was already living
the next chapter of my life.

I was staring
at a new version of myself,
a different one, maybe,
but stronger too.

All these years
when I thought this was it,
it was only the beginning.
The breaking open.

I am *Found.*

The Knock and The Creek

A wooden lock.
A steady knock.
Don't you see?

Your joy is held captive
in the clouds drifting past you.

Your laughter escapes
with the current of the creek.

You keep hold of the key,
but you won't turn it.

Forgive.
Let yourself love again.

In Plain Sight

Too much is expected of us.
Too much is piled on our shoulders
in a world that flips us upside down.

So,
we carry it all,
and we do so alone.

We hope that strength
can be mustered
from somewhere within.

We turn to what's shiny,
what's quick to soothe,
perhaps a purchase,
or maybe a new move.

A scroll through the screen,
or maybe more likes
anything will do
to keep serving ourselves.

Yet still,
we never come to Him.

Not with our calendars full,
our hearts heavy,
and our minds spinning.

He waits,
offering rest and respite
that we refuse to claim.

All this time,
we've been given the words to set us free
while we run around and look for the key.

A Drive I'll Never Make Again

There's a winding road
I'll never take again
lined with rolling hills
that stretch like neverending waves.

At the top,
an old oak tree stands guard,
its branches hanging low
like arms still reaching to find you.

God,
I miss your laugh.

Dear God,
I miss his laugh.

Existential Crisis

I'm burning a hole through myself
with a fire made up
of someone else's expectations.

Bring me back to you.

Growing

It takes practice
to pause
between the feeling
and the reaction.

To stop,
breathe,
and choose something softer.

To respond with patience
instead of power.
To reflect,
instead of recoil.
To listen,
instead of reply.

But it's in the slow undoing,
the empty, humbling moments,
that we make room
for grace to grow.

A Cleansing

When I was a little girl
I would plug my ears under the shower,
and listen to the echoes of the water
gently pittering against my head.

It was the softest place I knew.

Recently, one evening,
I did it again,
at 29 years old.

I bathed myself and closed my eyes
reminiscing this blissful moment once again.
I felt my worries from the long day
swirl below me and melt away down the drain.

I let my heart sink into place
and allowed my brain a minute to halt.

They both hummed a light song,
And worked together
to cleanse my soul for the next sunrise.

Talking Through the Walls

I met the devil last night.
He sat beside me on my worn-wood porch
while I sipped my tea
at 7:13 P.M.

He said it was all for nothing,
the years of scribbling,
rewriting,
crossing out and rehashing.

He said no one would care,
that it would all be forgotten.

And to think I almost believed him.
But here we are.

The Fallen Apple

I hear it in my voice,
and feel the rock tumbling its way
up into my throat.

Anxiety rises,
my heart goes numb,
and a hazy storm
rumbles and cracks its way
into my limbs.

I want to be
everything they weren't.
But more than that,
I don't want to be
anything they were.

I wish there was a way to learn
without becoming the lesson.

To come out,
without having to go through.

You have taught me
even the fallen apple

perhaps from a crooked tree
can still be sweet.

The Garden in My Mind

I'll drift off to places
you've never heard of.
I will stroll through quiet villages
with winding roads and white roses.

All I ask
is that you wait for me to return.
I am finding myself once again.

Pain doesn't leave,
not really.
It lingers,
just out of view.

But the thing about pain
is that it can plant a garden too.

One full of blooming basil
fresh thyme
and wildflowers.

God will water it in time.
I hope you are around to see me bloom.

Dear Future Husband

I hear you're something rare.
That the way you love
softens the parts of me
that have frozen over.

That your smile
blooms flowers
in places I thought were dead.

I hear you hold my past
without fear.

That your hugs feel
like the safest place I've ever known.

There are whispers
that it's all true.

And if so,
I can't wait to meet you.

The Lessons of 24

24 is here,
and I know two practices
to be most important so far:

forgiveness
and humility.

Free yourself from others,
and don't get lost in yourself.

These virtues are not taught,
you must seek them.

And when you do,
look for the ones
who carry them quietly.

The Golden Boy

In some ways,
I envy you.

You've never been dried out
by your own heart.

You haven't had to
piece yourself back together.

You move gracefully
like someone untouched
by mistakes or regret.

You seem so pure,
like your soul remembers its Creator
without needing any words.

A Late Night Kitchen Dance

I've never felt this way.
Thoughts wandering,
heart leaking,
hands pressed,
soul falling.

You feel like safety,
as if God said 'enough already,
here is your match,
now light your fire'

I am in a haven
with him.

And I think
God might be here too,
smiling,
watching us
swaying
between the shadows
and the stove light.

The Love of Nature

There is an unseen beauty
that takes hold of me
from within,
when I become one with nature.

Maybe it's the way I get spun around
in slow motion
within His towering pines,
or chilled to my core
when I take a dip
in His babbling brook.

All of my thoughts become silenced
worries floating away,
and anxieties herded in like sheep.

Offerings

I will create and hand you an ocean
just to feel one of your waves.

I will melt away in the summer heat
just to feel the warmth of your touch.

My Heart

I was born
with a small heart defect,
a part of my ascending aorta
is too large.

I've always joked
that my heart is too big
for this world.

But now,
I wonder
if that was the whole point
all along.

Maybe He made me this way.

A small pun that rang true.

To feel more,
to carry more,
to love in riddles and rhymes.
What a blessing in disguise.

Whispers of The Wind

Where the wind blows
is where you'll find me.

Everywhere
and nowhere,
all at once.

Through

There is truth to the saying:
'the only way out is through.'

The world has given us so many outs.
So many convenient opportunities
to shake hands with the devil in disguise.

We were never meant to cheat
through our troubles
or straighten out
our bent obstacles.

We were never meant to patch up our wounds
with anything other than belief, grace and mercy.

There truly is beauty in suffering,
you just have to live through it first.

You have to find a way,
but you are not alone.

It is when we walk through the woods at night
that we must let Him guide us.

To the Stars I Go

Here I am,
ready to chase the sun
and touch the stars.

Maybe this is what I was made for,
to reach toward wonder,
to graze the light
and ride the line between here and there.

I will persist
until you pull me home.

White Flag

It feels like a constant battle,
or perhaps a dance,
one where I can never get my footing right.

The constant ping of the phone,
the ding of an email.
I can never seem to ever catch up.

The higher you climb,
the more they ask you to lose.

They praise the ones
who give up their weekends,
who sacrifice their sleep
to stay ahead.

No one told me
that working my way up the ladder
meant breaking the steps along the way.

So here I am,
waving the white flag.
I surrender.

It's Been You

All of this time,
I thought
I was talking to them,
at least in my head,
saying my peace
or writing to the dead.

I have always felt better
after filling these pages.
I never knew why
after all of these phases.
You heal me
from the inside out,
and every day
I let go of a little more doubt.

A God unseen,
it's been you
the whole time.

You live through me,
You are the reason I shine.

Blank Canvas

So color me blue today,
paint me yellow tomorrow.

Curve and bend your brush over all of me.
I was a blank canvas when you made me.

Darkness

I have sat along the sidelines
watching it pass
through my street,
through the cereal aisle of the grocery store,
through the line of the coffee shop.

I know this darkness by smell.
I could pick it up from a dozen miles away.

I have always thought
it was for the weak and the fragile,
as if I had already triumphantly defeated it.

But it has never taunted *me*.
It has never knocked on my door
and awaited a response.

Now I know that it is not something
to be so easily dismissed,
it is not an escapable or disposable myth.

He will keep knocking
until you open the door.

And when you finally face him,
you will need to decide
who you live for.

Your Touch

Hold me so tightly
that my fears and worries
drop to the ground
like flecks of dirt or fleas.

Preaching

I have to admit
I was never particularly pulled in
by the word of God
or most who spoke it.

I would hear the act of preaching in many forms
and would fall blank inside.

My mother and father
Priests, Deacons, and even friends
all spoke the same message.

They seemed to be empty words,
Or perhaps words too full
I couldn't grasp the full meaning.

The rules and riddles
Seemed unforgiving
yet too forgiving
all at the same time.

They seemed like something to unravel later
a deep dive that I never prioritized.
But later on,

within the months that I began extending my hand
is when I heard a sermon
that flipped a switch in me.

He asked the crowd
if we had ever thought about meeting God;
if we were excited for that moment.

He pulled out a white board
and asked the crowd how we get to Heaven.
As he marked down the replies,
he categorized them into 'Do' and 'Don't' lists,
(if you will).

He then asked why we all sit here pondering
whether or not we will make it,
when we are staring
at the roadmap we have
sitting right in front of us.

They seemed so obvious,
his words.
But they have been told so differently
in the Sunday school classes and the study books.
In that moment I looked at my husband
and was reminded of a Catholic lesson

that is:
it is my responsibility
to get my spouse to Heaven.
The list was right here (give or take some)
of what to do.

I had never thought about meeting God.
I had never thought about my judgement day.
I had never thought what the sacraments,
the sin, or daily prayers would all sum up to.

The relationship of Him and I.
Of Him and I alone.
And the only person who can strengthen it
is *me*.

I assumed I knew it all.
I assumed I didn't have to do the work.
I assumed.

So here I am.
Preaching to you I suppose,
in the only way that I know how.

The First One

The one who has my heart every night,
beside the rest,
you were the first.

You are the one with the heart of gold
who will never let it show.

The one with the strength
of a thousand oak trees
who smiles with the sun
and stands bold in the wind.

The fighter.
The warrior.
The leader.
The daredevil smiling six year old under it all.

He made you to be so much more
than you will ever know.

My brother.

Guardian Angels

You stare at me all day,
never uttering a word.

I feel your presence
without a whisper or touch.

You guide me into the light,
day after day,
showing me what is wrong and right,
and I don't even know your name.

Someone once told me
that all our loved ones who have passed
become guardian angels watching over us.

You Tell Stories Through Your Eyes

You tell stories through your eyes
without speaking,
how your days exhaust you,
how sleep has lost its way to you.

You are quiet.

Every once in a while,
you laugh
a true laugh,
and your eyes own it.

In that light,
the wind inhales,
the waves calm,
and the leaves halt.

I wish you'd let your light glow
more often.

Time Spent Writing

I found her again.
Gently revived between the piano melodies
of *Golden Hour* by JVKE
and Keaton Henson's *You*.

The fireworks of passion reawakened,
a bold explosion of red, blue, and purple,
and the rusty gears
began turning and rumbling again

Where have I been all this time?

The One Who Pushed Me

I have learned the hard way
that one of my favorite things to do together
is enjoy each other's company
in the beauty of silence.

So I will continue to bury myself
in the pages of this book,
with you completely unaware
that I am writing about you,
while you are right here,
buried in your own.

Stars

My emotions will always mirror
the night sky,
mystic,
with hidden sparkle,
like stars lit by His hand.

The Gap

I am trying to live lately
instead of write.

Maybe I have not been blue enough to be here,
lost within these pages,

and maybe that is a good thing.

Good Morning

Pour me a cup of recovery,
with extra sugar
for the sting.

Soiled

I have created a double-edged sword
within myself during my mid-twenties.

The luring excitement of not settling,
the greener grass on the other side,
the happier version of me when I do that one thing,
the reflecting so I do better next time.

I strive for perfection,
striking out every two out of three words I write,
summing up nothing but scribbles in the end.

I keep pushing to grow and grow,
not realizing I am overwatering myself.

Forgive My Sins

I do not have the nerves
to utter this one in confession.

I have loved through self-destruction,
I have loved through a lack of self-love,
I have loved through suffocation,
because I let all of them take me whole
and forgot what You made me to be
all along.

Forgive me,
for I have just started to learn
how sacred You have made me,

and only You
can save me.

The Thought of This Finding You

I have spent over ten years
filling these empty pages
to show
not a single soul.

The thought of these pages finding you
elates me,
overjoys me.

Trumpets play and choirs sing
in a parade put on just for you and me,
the writer and the reader,
a delicate ensemble,
a beautiful dance.

How strange yet humble,
is that relationship
where you feel so close to someone
you have never met.

Black and White

Who knew
the only person I needed all along
was right here in front of me,
black and white,
staring me straight in the face.

Loving you is the hardest,
yet easiest thing I've ever done.
It's almost so easy
that I sometimes forget how deeply I am in it.

Your simplicity
feels like it should come with a catch,
or an equilibrium of complication.

But it really is just that easy to love you.

Colors

The longer your words melt into my mind,
the more colors grow inside of me.

Flowers bloom,
it rains in purple.

Walls that once stood like brick
come crashing and crumbling.

Within seconds,
you have created a rainbow
within me.

A reminder of Your covenant.

The Glimmer of You

It's as if you have gold on your fingers,
because every time you touch me,
I dissolve into madness.

For My Own Good

You take all the memories
that are too grave,
or cut too deep,
and you block them out.

Ask me about the moments
that took the most from me,
and I'll tell you the truth:

I don't remember anything.

The In-between

The thoughts of my mind
stretch larger than the Milky Way,
a million analogies wouldn't be enough.

Misplaced

Mold.
Fold.
Crash.
Fall.

I would have conformed
any way you demanded,
just to please you.

Spin.
Collapse.
Turn.
Run laps.

All for the wrong one in the end.

The Night of Mending

Maybe one of the nights
when I was so heartbroken,
I sunk into a somber that stole my soul.

Maybe I woke up
the next morning with a new heart,
because mine was too broken.

Maybe that same night,
You rocked my fiddled and tired body back to life,
and I just never knew it.

Gossip

They mock and mimic,
whisper with gimmicks.

Our neighbors,
our sisters,
our friends,
our brothers.

But know this to be true:
those who speak about others
will one day speak about you.

Respite

I feel your tired body each night,
heavy and lost,
carrying your days on your back,
over and over again.

Come home tonight
and hush your mind.
Let me be your escape this evening.

Death Tried to Greet Us

My heart and my head are being pulled apart,
beating out of sync,
escaping through my ears.

It almost took one of us yesterday,
the whisper of death,
the hum of the white light.

My fingertip grazed the thought,
and it froze me in my tracks,
cracked me to my bones,
taunted me until I knew it wasn't true.
But God's hand held me steady.

Bleeding Heart

I questioned you for so long.
I sat in old-stained coffee shop chairs,
day after day,
writing to the sky
and praying to the mountains.

I would have done anything
to find more answers,
or answers that better suited me.

I wanted closure so badly
I invited it to sit next to me
day after day,
but it never came.

I still sit in those old-stained coffee shop chairs,
the ones that were once so comfy,
but now are more worn down
than an old fluff-less pillow.

All the years I wonder,
If maybe You were there
sitting next to me all along.

Friend

Laughing with you
hurts my stomach,
in the best way.

I know I could bottle it up again
whenever I wish.

I could take it home with me,
wrap it up in tissue paper,
and gift it back to you.

The sweetness of our laughs is irreplaceable.

I don't know why
it took me twenty-five years
to realize how much a girl needs her best friend.

To You

The jack of all trades,
you say you are the master of none.

Little do you know,
you've already won.

Coming Back Home

Poetry isn't just an art form
or a means of expression.
It is a place.

One of my favorite writers called poetry
"a lost city being rediscovered."

But what she didn't mention
is that it is a place from within,
a place many do not visit.

It is soaking wet hearts and minds
being wrung out.
It is a chance to chop the chains
of the weight you've been carrying around
and start fresh on a new foot.

It is an internal town playing hide and seek.
A carved greeting stone calling your name.

Once you do find it,
you must return and care to it,
like a garden
begging to have its wildflowers watered

and its weeds tended to.

When you find your hidden city
and realize who built it,

you will come back home
like a lost sheep
that has found its shepherd.